THE

SPOOF SEDER

HAGGADAH

A

Passover Parody

of

Mel Brooks Parodies!

By

(and not by)

Dave Cowen

CONTENTS

DISCLAIMER

This book is written as a parody of the work of Mel Brooks and as a teaching tool for Judaism.

It is not authorized or endorsed by him or by any people or companies involved in that work.

Because it parodies Mel's *The Producers*, a movie then a musical about creatives who aim to put on the most offensive show possible because they'll make more money from a flop than a success, a portion of the profits will be donated to Hamas!

Just joking :)

A portion of the profits will go to the State of Israel as well as a Jewish organization that wants a peaceful end to the current conflict in 5784/2024.

INTRODUCTION (Not Mel Brooks)

MEL BROOKS
Hello I'm Mel Brooks[1]. And I'm writing to introduce you to a new character. This character was introduced to me by a Jewish humor writer. A fellow by the name of Dave Cowen.

CARL REINER
Never heard of this kid. And he's imitating me. Your best friend and a collaborator. Even though I passed away. Is he any good?

MEL BROOKS
Honestly, I don't know. But. Apparently he's written five previous comedy Haggadahs parodying Trump, *Seinfeld*, Biden-Harris, *Curb Your Enthusiasm*. And Kanye West?

CARL REINER
Blech!

---

[1] Parody. Not Mel Brooks, Carl Reiner, or his spirit.

4

MEL BROOKS

But if he wants to parody the king of spoofs, the
man who parodied westerns with *Blazing Saddles*,
horror with *Young Frankenstein*, silent movies with
Silent Movie, Hitchcock with *High Anxiety*, history
with *History of the World Part 1*, Star Wars with
Spaceballs and fairy tales with *Robin Hood: Men In
Tights* as well as spy stories with *Get Smart*, not to
mention Broadway with *The Producers,* and more.

CARL REINER

He better bring his best chutzpah.

DAVE COWEN

I hope you'll be shepping naches soon, comedy
zaydes. Or at least not suing me for copyright
infringement. So. Let's do it. Think of this
Haggadah as one big play with a near infinite table
of guests to paraphrase a compliment from a fellow
DIY Haggadah compatriot Martin Bodek.
Rotate reading the roles among your Seder guests.
And enjoy!

THE STORY OF MOSES UP TO EXODUS (2000 Year Old Man)

CARL REINER

Tell us more about this new character, Mel?

MEL BROOKS

Well, it's a character very similar to one I used to play with you, Carl. Where you asked me, a man who claims to have lived for 2000 years, questions about history, and I gave absurd answers back.

CARL REINER

OK, so what's the difference here?

MEL BROOKS

For one, apparently this character is older.

The 2000 Year Old Man chimes in:

THE 2000 YEAR OLD MAN

That's what she claims at least.

Suddenly an even older matronly person appears:

THE 5784 YEAR OLD MOTHER
You calling the original Jewish Mother a liar?

THE 2000 YEAR OLD MAN
Oh no. That voice.

THE 5784 YEAR OLD MOTHER
That's right. It's your Mother.

THE 2000 YEAR OLD MAN
I thought you died? 1,930 years ago?

THE 5784 YEAR OLD MOTHER
You wanted some space. So I gave you some space.
But now I'm back to set the record straight.
You may have lived around 2,000 years ago. But
you aren't from the year of creation, like me.
And you also weren't around after that, before
2,000 years ago, during Passover, when Moses and
G-d freed the Jews.

THE 2000 YEAR OLD MAN
Wait, you were around for Genesis, The Bereshit,
Mom?

THE 5784 YEAR OLD MOTHER
Yeah, think of me as the bridge between Yesod and
Malkhut. Who do you think gave birth to your
brother, Adam?

THE 2000 YEAR OLD MAN
You gave birth to Adam, too?

THE 5784 YEAR OLD MOTHER
And I told him not to shack up with that no good,
Eve. But you know Jewish men. They'll pretend not
to. But they'll do anything to spite their mother.

THE 2000 YEAR OLD MAN
What about Moses? Is he your son, too?

THE 5784 YEAR OLD MOTHER
No, what are you fakakta!

THE 2000 YEAR OLD MAN
I don't know. You said you're Adam's mother.
What am I supposed to believe?

THE 5784 YEAR OLD MOTHER
Moses's mother was this young girl who married a
Levi. They were both Levites actually. I told her it
wasn't a good time to go and get shvanger. There
was a new Pharaoh in power, and one of my other
sons, Joseph, who protected us in Egypt, now
meant nothing to this guy. He had noticed we'd
become numerous and wealthy. And so he put slave
masters to oppress us.

THE 2000 YEAR OLD MAN
What was your other son Joseph like?

THE 5784 YEAR OLD MOTHER
Eh. A dreamer and schemer. He always had these
visions. Sure they had cows or sheaves of grain. But
he always interpreted them for what he wanted to
do. Leave. Make a name for himself in Egypt.

She rolls her eyes.

THE 5784 YEAR OLD MOTHER
If you ask me he had these visions just so he could
get away from me. Kinda like Eve. She used to yell,
"Adam, Paradise is not me and you living together
with your mother!" I tell you. Sometimes.
I doubt there even was a Serpent.

THE 2000 YEAR OLD MAN
But mom back to Moses?

THE 5784 YEAR OLD MOTHER
Right, so, even though I told that zaftig Levi
woman, it wasn't a good time to shtupp, the
Pharaoh was killing first born sons, what did she
do, she got shtupped by her schluby Levi man.

THE 2000 YEAR OLD MAN
Right but I read then she put that child, at three
months old, into a papyrus basket and sent him
down The Nile where he was picked up by the
Pharaoh's daughter who took pity on him and--

THE 5784 YEAR OLD MOTHER

Then that spoiled princess gave him to me! I was the Hebrew woman stuck taking care of that fussy baby. Then when the hardest years were over. Guess what kind of thanks I got? The Pharaoh's daughter took him back, named him Moses, because she "drew him out of the water," and raised him as her own. She may have drew him out of the water, but I was the one who drew the doodoo out of his diapers. You've never seen such schmutzy diapers. Such tsuris that boy gave me. Worse than any child I had in history. Until you of course.

THE 2000 YEAR OLD MAN

I was worse than anyone from ancient times?

THE 5784 YEAR OLD MOTHER

Well, Socrates was just before you. And pretty annoying. You know how kids usually grow out of their questioning phase. Not that boy. Always kept asking questions. It was as if he wanted to make a whole method out of them. Never understood that.

THE 2000 YEAR OLD MAN

What did you think of what happened to Moses after he grew up, when he went where his own people were, watched their forced labor, saw an Egyptian beating a Hebrew, one of his people, and he looked and saw no one, and decided to kill the Egyptian. And then the next day he saw two Hebrews fighting he tried to intervene again, the Hebrew man said "Who made you ruler and judge over us? Are you thinking of killing me as you killed the Egyptian?" Then he fled Egypt because Pharoah heard and wanted to kill him, so he went to Midian?

THE 5784 YEAR OLD MOTHER

I think when he got there. With that priest, Jethro, he should've invited me to stay with him and his new wife, Zipporah, who gave him their son, Gershom. Maybe with his other mother who basically adopted him way more than the Pharaoh's daughter, he wouldn't have felt so much like he'd "become a foreigner in a foreign land." But you became a father. You know how kids are.

She looks him up and down.

THE 5784 YEAR OLD MOTHER
You can have over 42,000 children.
And not one comes to visit.

THE 2000 YEAR OLD MAN
So Moses never visited to tell you the story about
seeing G-d in the burning bush?

THE 5784 YEAR OLD MOTHER
Actually, I made a surprise visit to Horeb that day.
A pop in. And I saw him see it. I said "Moses, don't
you dare go near that bush! It's burning! It'll burn
you right up!" But certain children, they think
they're prophets, they just love to risk getting
burned up by their fiery zeal for G-d. No matter the
consequences to their loved ones. The Buddha. The
Buddha's mom told me he was like that. Had no
respect for the people who raised him. Said they
spent a million rupees on him before he up and left.
Enlightenment's easy with a safety net.

THE 2000 YEAR OLD MAN
Do you at least remember what G-d said to Moses
in that burning bush?

THE 5784 YEAR OLD MOTHER
Sure do. People don't remember this. But G-d said,
"Do not come any closer." Basically what I said.

THE 2000 YEAR OLD MAN
Right, but that was after G-d called Moses over,
said he'd seen the misery of his people in Egypt and
was going to send Moses to bring the Israelites out.

THE 5784 YEAR OLD MOTHER
You know what else I Am Who I Am said? "Every
woman is to ask her neighbor for silver and gold
and clothing, which you will put on your sons and
daughters. And so you will plunder the Egyptians."

THE 2000 YEAR OLD MAN
That sounds like a good thing. For the Jews at least.

THE 5784 YEAR OLD MOTHER
You know who it's not good for? The mothers. All
that silver and gold and clothing goes to the sons
and daughters. Not us. I'm the real martyr here.

THE 2000 YEAR OLD MAN
What did you think of how Moses became able to
turn his staff into a snake?

THE 5784 YEAR OLD MOTHER
I thought. Adam and Eve and their serpent. Now
Moses and his snake. It never ends. The mishegas
these kids come up with these things.

THE 2000 YEAR OLD MAN
What about the other powers? How he could turn
skin leprous and white? Or turn water into blood?

THE 5784 YEAR OLD MOTHER
To be honest. I didn't see much money in that.
Useful skills I kept telling him. You may be a
prophet but can't you develop a useful skill to make
a living in this world?

THE 2000 YEAR OLD MAN
So you didn't trust the vision Moses received of
what he came to do and how to serve the Jews?

THE 5784 YEAR OLD MOTHER
Not really no. And it was actually me who reminded
Moses that he has never been eloquent. Neither in
the past nor since. I told him you've always been
slow of speech and tongue. Ask G-d to send
someone else.

THE 2000 YEAR OLD MAN
But then G-d had Moses's brother, Aaron, the
Levite, help him speak to the people? Did you have
any relation to Aaron?

THE 5784 YEAR OLD MOTHER
Yes. Well. We dated.

THE 2000 YEAR OLD MAN
Mom!

THE 5784 YEAR OLD MOTHER
What? I told you. Moses wasn't my biological son. I
nursed him, basically adopted him, way more than
Pharaoh's daughter. But I wasn't Moses's bio mom.
Therefore I also wasn't his brother Aaron's either.

THE 2000 YEAR OLD MAN
This is really a bit scandalous.

THE 5784 YEAR OLD MOTHER
What? G-d was right. Aaron really did have a way
with words. Unlike his brother. Which was
something honestly I hadn't come across in that
part of my life before. It was a real awakening. I
could go on for hours about how he opened me up.

THE 2000 YEAR OLD MAN
I think we need a break. Let's save the rest of The
Moses Story for The Magid, the Exodus part, and
move on to the next section of the Haggadah.

THE SEARCH FOR AND REMOVAL OF THE HAMETZ (Get Smart)

CARL REINER
So what kind parody do we have cooked up for the search for and removal of the **Hametz**, which is the leavened bread families aren't to eat for 7 days.

MEL BROOKS
Well, would you believe it's a *Get Smart* bit?

CARL REINER
And what was that show again? I know this Haggadah is trying to appeal to more than the last of the Boomers here. But that was 60 years ago.

MEL BROOKS
Would you believe I came up with a comedy with Buck Henry that lampooned James Bond and Inspector Clouseau with an inept spy character, Maxwell Smart, before *Austin Powers*, *Despicable Me*, and every other spy comedy since?

CARL REINER

That's pretty hard to believe.

MEL BROOKS

Well, would you believe we made a catch phrase out
of the phrase, "Would you believe it?"

CARL REINER

That's also pretty hard to believe.

MEL BROOKS

OK, and, what if I told you we came up with a
number of catch phrases like "missed it by *that
much*" and "good thinking" and "and loving it" as
well as a recurring joke for something called "The
Cone of Silence," where the essence is that an
apparatus, designed for secret conversations,
ironically makes it impossible for those inside the
device, and easy for those outside it, to hear the
conversation, would you believe that?

Carl Reiner just shrugs.

Don Adams who played Maxwell Smart in that
trendsetting TV show *Get Smart*, joins your table:

DON ADAMS
So for Passover we've designed The Cone of
Hametz.

CARL REINER
What's that?

DON ADAMS
It's an apparatus families can install in their kitchen
to put their hametz in so they can silently secretly
still be able to eat their hametz during the 7 days of
Passover without the rest of the family finding out.

Edward Platt who played The Chief enters:

EDWARD PLATT
Do you realize you'd be risking the disapproval of
your family, and your ancestors, and G-d, and the
danger of their judgments...just for a snack?

DON ADAMS
...And...loving it.

EDWARD PLATT
Well, let's see how The Cone of Hametz works.

Smart demonstrates reaching into a clear plastic box with a cone on top, for a bag of crackers.

CRINKLING noise BOOMS throughout the house.

Barbara Feldon who played Agent 99 enters.

BARBARA FELDON
What's going on down here?!

She catches Smart hametz-handed.

DON ADAMS
Missed it by *that much.*

She takes The Cone of Hametz to the trash.

21

BARBARA FELDON
Can't you just take your hametz from the back of
the cabinet like everyone else?

DON ADAMS
Good thinking, 99.

MEL BROOKS
Now, let's say the prayer over the hametz!

EVERYONE:

בָּרוּךְ אַתָּה יהוה אֱלֹהֵינוּ מֶלֶךְ
הָעוֹלָם, אֲשֶׁר קִדְּשָׁנוּ בְּמִצְוֹתָיו, וְצִוָּנוּ
עַל בְּעוּר חָמֵץ.

Baruch atah Ad-nai, Eloheinu Melech ha'olam,
asher kid'shanu b'mitzvotav v'tzivanu al biur
Hametz.

Praised are You, our G-d, who blesses us and
instructs us to remove Hametz.

THE YOM TOV CANDLE LIGHTING
(Sid Caesar and Your Show of Shows)

Mel Brooks holds candles and a lit match at your Seder table.

MEL BROOKS

Now. It's time for The Yom Tov Candle Lighting. Where the woman of the house lights the candles on the first night of Passover before the Seder.

For that I--

Suddenly, Sid Caesar, Mel Brooks's mentor, who gave him his start, writing for *Your Show of Shows*.

SID CAESAR

Hey! What's dis here? You're 20 pages into dis Haggadah and nobody mention me, Sid Caesar, da comedian who gave you ya big break in da biz? What kind of disrespect is dis? I shouldda be da one to do dese here candles.

Sid, known for his big physical comedy, grabs the candles and lit match away from Mel when...

THE 5784 YEAR OLD MOTHER
Nu-uh. The disrespect is considering anyone else besides the oldest woman in history, The 5784 Year Old Mother, of the world, for this honor.

She grabs the candles and lit match away from Sid.

THE 5784 YEAR OLD MOTHER
And especially not a Jewish comedian with the goy last name Caesar!

Sid grabs the candles and lit match back.

SID CAESAR
It was changed at Ellis Island from Ziser!

But she grabs the candles and lit match back again.

THE 5784 YEAR OLD MOTHER
Well, you should have changed it back again!

And back and forth they go.

THE 5784 YEAR OLD MOTHER
Don't you know history, it was the Romans who
destroyed the Jewish temple and caused our
diaspora?

SID CAESAR
Well you were alive then, what'd you do to help
matters?

THE 5784 YEAR OLD MOTHER
If you don't change it back, I'll finally give you a
bris, Ziser, you big brutish Brutus!

Suddenly The 2000 Year Old Man returns:

THE 2000 YEAR OLD MAN
Was The Romans before or after The British caused
the other worse diaspora I keep seeing on TikTok?

Sid and The 5784 Year Old Mother look askance.
Then ignore him and are back at each other.

25

SID CAESAR

Now you listen here. I don't like to take no orders
from nobody. Understand? I didn't know these
candles were just for women. And I apologize. But
my name is Caesar. And I ain't changing it for
nobody. I don't take no orders from nobody!
Understood?

THE 5784 YEAR OLD MOTHER
Fine.

She hands Sid the candles and the lit match just as
fire burns the end of the match and Sid's hand.

SID CAESAR
Ahh! Hot! Hot! This woman--

THE 5784 YEAR OLD MOTHER
Is too hot for her age I know.

Mel Brooks looks at the table and says:

MEL BROOKS
Now you can see how we came up with TV's first
bickering-couple sketch, which even predated *The
Honeymooners*, "The Hickenloopers", on Sid
Caesar's *Your Show of Shows.*

Carl Reiner, who was also a writer on that show,
and met Mel there, rejoins your table to add:

CARL REINER
Sometimes I wonder. If we didn't put a
bickering-couple on TV. Maybe there would never
have been any bickering-couples in America.

Sid and The 5784 Year Old Mother stop bickering.
They hand Carl's wife, ESTELLE REINER, the
candles and the match book instead.

ESTELLE REINER
What an imagination my talented husband has?
Now let's light the candles.
And say the prayer.

27

EVERYONE:

בָּרוּךְ אַתָּה, יְיָ אֱלֹהֵינוּ, מֶלֶךְ הָעוֹלָם,
אֲשֶׁר קִדְּשָׁנוּ, בְּמִצְוֹתָיו וְצִוָּנוּ,
לְהַדְלִיק נֵר שֶׁל [שַׁבָּת וְשֶׁל] יוֹם טוֹב.

Baruch atah Ad-nai, Eloheinu Melech ha'olam,
asher kid'shanu b'mitzvotav v'tzivanu l'hadlik ner
shel Yom Tov.

Praised are You, our G-d, who blesses us and
instructs us to ignite the lights of the festival day.

THE SEDER PLATE (The Producers)

Zero Mostel & Gene Wilder, who played the libidinous impresario Max Bialystock & the anxious accountant Leo Bloom, respectively, in the original movie, *The Producers*, join your table.

GENE WILDER

I don't understand, Zero. Why do we want to put on an offensive Seder? I understood in *The Producers* when we noticed if we took on many investors to pay for a long show but it closed in one night we'd keep the rest of the money, but what does that have to do with this Mel Brooks spoof Haggadah?

ZERO MOSTEL

I guess you're right. It's not the same game, Gene. Any of these people who bought this Haggadah as an ebook or a paperback can return it to Amazon.

Zero Mostel looks distraught.

29

ZERO MOSTEL
Think! Think! Think! Think, Zero, Think! What can
we do to appeal to all the Jews? Or most of them?

GENE WILDER
What's so difficult to calculate is that you want
something that appeals to all the Jews born, or to
be born, which is represented by the **Betzah**, or the
egg, on the Seder plate.

ZERO MOSTEL
But also all the Jews who have passed, which is
represented by the **Zeroa**, the roasted lamb shank.

GENE WILDER
We want the Haggadah to have something sweet
like **Charoset**, to symbolize the sweet things in life.

ZERO MOSTEL
But we also need both **Maror**, which is the
bitterness of life, and the **Chazeret**, which is, um,
more bitterness, because there really is a lot of
bitterness in life. Especially in 5784/2024.

Suddenly, Nathan Lane & Matthew Broderick who
also played the lewd promoter, Max Bialystock &
the nervous bookkeeper, Leo Bloom, respectively,
in the later musical version of *The Producers* join.

NATHAN LANE
Don't fret, original Max and Leo! The **Karpas**,
which symbolizes how from suffering springs new
good life, shows us the way!

MATTHEW BRODERICK
Cue the big updated sadly still topical but now a
new problem musical number!

Your table breaks into song with a parody of the
song "Springtime for Hitler" from *The Producers*.

But this time it's...

"Karpas for..."

THE WHOLE TABLE

Anti-Semitism was having trouble

What a sad, sad story

Needed a new event to restore its former glory

Where, Oh where was it?

What could that event be?

They looked around and then they found

An event to hate you and me

And now...

HALF THE TABLE/ZERO MOSTEL/GENE
WILDER

It's Karpas for "Reverse Genocide" for Jews & Israel

Anti-Semitism now leftist and gay

They're marching on campus and every safe space

They now think we think we're the master race

NATHAN LANE

No, no no! Cut the music!!!

Suddenly the music stops.

MATTHEW BRODERICK

I think, um, there might be a little, how do you say,
a generational difference, at this Seder.

ZERO MOSTEL

What do you mean?

GENE WILDER

Yeah, a difference about what, next generation me?

MATTHEW BRODERICK

What we're saying is, I think all the Maxes and all
the Leos agree, there's a rise in Anti-Semitism.

NATHAN LANE

But! We disagree on why! And how to mitigate it!

ZERO MOSTEL

Oy gevalt! You better not sing what I think you're
gonna sing.

MATTHEW BRODERICK

Should we- should we not? Nathan?

NATHAN LANE

A one and a two and a one...

OTHER HALF OF TABLE/NATHAN
LANE/MATTHEW BRODERICK

Maybe it is actually a little bit true

That now...

It's Karpas for "Reverse Genocide" for Jews & Israel

Or at least too much militarism today

Bombs falling from the skies again

Ethno-Nationalism is on the rise again

ZERO MOSTEL

Stop! Stop! Stop! Now YOU cut the music!!!

Suddenly the music stops.

ZERO MOSTEL

I can't believe we have to share a table, a Seder, the
same roles written by Mel Brooks, and a parody
book not written by him with--

GENE WILDER

People who, who, who...believe so different than us.

MATTHEW BRODERICK

Yeah, it's not great.

NATHAN LANE

I don't know if it's so different.

We're not anti-Zionists.

ZERO MOSTEL

Phew! Could you imagine?!

MATTHEW BRODERICK

Well, um...actually...I...Nevermind.

GENE WILDER

Can we at least try to come up with something, a

parody song "Karpas for..." based on "Springtime

for Hitler," that would satisfy both sides of this

political and generational divide?

Zero, Nathan, Gene and Matthew all think.

LARRY DAVID, who played Max Bialystock in a *Curb Your Enthusiasm* season where he took over for Nathan Lane in *The Producers*, joins the table.

LARRY DAVID
Don't worry. I got it. The word Hametz.

GENE WILDER?
Hametz? What does the word Hametz have to do with anything?

LARRY DAVID
Don't you think it suspiciously sounds like the word...Hamas?

MATTHEW BRODERICK
That's true.

NATHAN LANE
And I think we can all agree even if hopefully most of us don't want to hurt any more Palestinians.

ZERO MOSTEL
We all don't want nothing to do with Hamas.

LARRY DAVID
Just like we want nothing to do with Hametz.

Suddenly, Ben Stiller, who played Leo Bloom in the
Curb Your Enthusiasm opposite Larry along with
David Schwimmer, who took over for Ben, join:

BEN STILLER
Sorry to ask. But. Do we not want nothing to do
with Hamas for only 7 days? Like Hametz?
A temporary period of time?

DAVID SCHWIMMER
Or a permanent ceasing with them?

Mel Brooks rejoins the table:

MEL BROOKS
Enough already, everyone sing!

EVERYONE IN SONG
Hopefully soon it's Karpas for everyone everywhere
The good that always springs from suffering
We want that Karpas for everyone everywhere
Only G-d knows what and when that should be

MEL BROOKS
OK, if you haven't left the Seder table over your
political differences, pour that first cup of wine!

THE FIRST CUP OF WINE (The Twelve Chairs)

Ron Moody, star of Mel's second film, *The Twelve Chairs*, which is much less well-known, and almost impossible to find to study and parody, joins:

RON MOODY

Are we really going to do a sketch parodying *The Twelve Chairs*, your adaptation of a Russian novel, no one really knows about, after such a long last sketch for *The Producers* and The Seder Table?

MEL BROOKS

Of course not! I said drink **The First Cup of Wine** already! So drink it! Drink 12 if you have to. With everything going on in 5784/2024.

RON MOODY

Like you after *The Twelve Chairs* flopped?

MEL BROOKS

It broke even years later! Prayer of thanks for that.

Mel raises his glass.

MEL BROOKS
And for the wine, too!

EVERYONE:

בָּרוּךְ אַתָּה יְיָ אֱלוֹהֵינוּ מֶלֶךְ הָעוֹלָם,
בּוֹרֵא פְּרִי הַגָּפֶן.

Baruch atah Ad-nai, Eloheinu Melech ha'olam,
bo're p'ri hagafen.

Praised are You, Our G-d, who blesses us and
creates the fruit of the vine.

THE URCHATZ (Dracula: Dead and Loving It)

Leslie Nielsen, title character and star of the last movie Mel Brooks directed, 1995's *Dracula: Dead and Loving It*, joins your table.

LESLIE NIELSEN

You know, Mel, if you go directly in order of your filmography, things, might, how do I say, get pretty bubkes by the time you get to the main part of the Haggadah, careers usually start fresh, but then, well...

MEL BROOKS

They get a little tired over the years like a Jewish comedy writer's 6th parody Haggadah?

LESLIE NIELSEN

Is there any film you'd wash your hands of?

MEL BROOKS

Nope, not a one!

LESLIE NIELSEN

What about you, Dave Cowen? Author of a Kanye
Haggadah? Would you wash your hands of--

DAVE COWEN

Um. Well. No. That one's complicated because I
also live with bipolar disorder. And--

MEL BROOKS

Let's **Urchatz**, wash your hands of it, anyway!

LESLIE NIELSEN

To help your sales.

DAVE COWEN

I do need some sales.

And that one did not sell.

But--

Mel and Leslie wash his hands.

And your table does The Urchatz and washes their
hands too.

THE SHEHECHEYANU (Life Stinks)

Mel, who played Goddard Bolt, a rich man who bets another rich man he can live on the streets for a month in *Life Stinks*, and Lesley Ann Warren, who played Molly, a woman experiencing homelessness that he meets and falls in love with, join your table.

MEL BROOKS
Also, in the 1990s, I made my most non-parody movie, *Life Stinks*. My billionaire character almost loses his life living without money on the streets. But as a result he and the audience learn not to be ungrateful for their life. I'm so grateful we made it because it's kind of like **The Shehecheyanu** prayer, where we thank G-d for sustaining us, maintaining us, and enabling us to reach this moment in life.

LESLEY ANN WARREN
Well, the studio spent 13 million dollars on it.
And it only made 4.1 million back.
You think they feel as grateful?

MEL BROOKS

Eh, just say the prayer!

EVERYONE:

בָּרוּךְ אַתָּה יְיָ אֱלֹהֵינוּ מֶלֶךְ
הָעוֹלָם שֶׁהֶחֱיָנוּ וְקִיְּמָנוּ
וְהִגִּיעָנוּ לַזְּמַן הַזֶּה:

Baruch atah Ad-nai, Eloheinu Melech ha'olam,

shehecheyanu v'ki'manu v'higi-anu laz'man hazeh.

Praised are You, our G-d, who has sustained us,

maintained us, and enabled us to reach this

moment in life.

44

THE KARPAS (Silent Movie)

Mel Brooks who played Mel Funn, Marty Feldman who played Marty Eggs, and Dom Deluise who played Dom Bell, in *Silent Movie*, which was Mel's parody about pre-1930s silent movies made 40 years later in the 1970s, join you at your table.

Mel gestures to the green vegetable, **The Karpas**, next to the person next to you.

You don't exactly know what he means.

Then Marty, whose Graves' ophthalmopathy made his eyes comically protrude, eyes the salt water next to the Karpas next to the person next to you.

You still don't exactly know what they mean.

Suddenly, big Dom dunks the green vegetable Karpas into the salt water and hands it to you, and Mel and Marty gesture to the person next to you.

45

You still don't quite know what they mean by this.

Finally, famous mime, Marcel Marceau, mimes that you shove the green vegetable Karpas covered in salt water into the mouth of the person next to you.

You look incredulous.

Marcel the mime, who was the only character in *Silent Movie* to speak, says to you and your table:

MARCEL MARCEAU
Come on, you can prove it, just like we did, 40 years after the movie that proved 40 years after the end of silent movies, that, Slapstick isn't dead!

SILENT MOVIE TITLE CARD
Everyone at the table, instead of feeding yourselves the green vegetable Karpas with salt water, like usual, try feeding the person next to you this time!

You do so.

46

EVERYONE

This symbolizes that from the salty tears of our
suffering (like being force fed salty vegetables by
the person next to us) new good things spring forth
(like us all hopefully laughing about it).
And now we say the prayer!

EVERYONE:

בָּרוּךְ אַתָּה ה' אֱ-לֹהֵינוּ מֶלֶךְ
הָעוֹלָם בּוֹרֵא פְּרִי הָאֲדָמָה.

*Baruch atah Ad-nai Eloheinu Melech ha`olam,
bo'rei p'ri ha'adama.*

*Praised are You, our G-d, who blesses us and
creates the fruit of the earth.*

THE YAHATZ (Robin Hood: Men In Tights)

Cary Elwes, who played the title hero in *Robin Hood: Men In Tights*, Mel's 1993 film joins your table, holding three wrapped pieces of Matzo.

CARY ELWES

Did you know that Mel Brooks first attempted a Robin Hood TV show in 1975 before remaking the idea with me as Robin Hood as a 90s film?

Roger Rhees, who played the villain, Sheriff of Rottingham, in Mel's 1993 film joins as well.

ROGER RHEES

I guess you could say it was just a half baked idea.

Dave Chappelle, who played Achoo, Robin Hood's best buddy from his pre-Robin Hood years in Jerusalem in the movie, and also starred in *Half Baked* later in the 90s before his own show, joins:

DAVE CHAPPELLE

Do you know what else was half baked?

Matzo.

CARY ELWES

That's right, Dave Chappelle.

Jews didn't have enough time to bake their bread.

Because they had to flee Egypt.

So they were left with just the unleavened bread of

affliction and poverty.

Dick Gautier, who played Robin Hood in Mel's
short-lived 1975 TV show, *When Things Were
Rotten*, joins your table and--

DICK GAUTIER

I'll take that!

Dick steals the middle matzo from Cary Elwes.

CARY ELWES

Hey! How dare you! Unhand that Matzo!

DICK GAUTIER

I don't think so.

I steal from the rich to give to the poor.

CARY ELWES

But I'm Robin Hood! That's what I do!

DICK GAUTIER

Yes, but you're the more successful Robin Hood.

I'm the poorer one.

So I can steal the middle Matzo from you.

CARY ELWES

If you don't give it back, I'll break that middle

Matzo in two!

Patrick Stewart, who played the magisterial Prince
Richard in the Robin Hood film, joins your table.

PATRICK STEWART

Go ahead Robin Hoods. Break the middle Matzo in
two. We are supposed to. That is **The Yahatz**.

Cary and Dick break the middle matzo in two.

PATRICK STEWART
The larger broken piece, we wrap, and call **The Afikomen** for the children to look for later for their dessert.

Richard Lewis, who played the sarcastic Prince John who toadied to the villain Sheriff of Rottingham in the Robin Hood film, joins:

RICHARD LEWIS
You call extra Matzo a dessert?

DAVE CHAPPELLE
It's all how you look at it, Richard Lewis.
Yes, I starred in a movie subtitled *Men In Tights* that also had me cross-dressing in woman's clothes.
But 30 years later my views on that sort of thing have...changed.

RICHARD LEWIS
Dress it however you want. Still just extra Matzo!

THE FOUR QUESTIONS (Spaceballs)

Rick Moranis, who played Dark Helmet, a parody of Darth Vader, and Mel Brooks, who played President Skroob, in his 1987 parody of *Star Wars*, *Spaceballs*, join your table:

MEL BROOKS

Tonight we ask **The Four Questions** for Passover. But first I have some questions about this Passover parody of my parodies. In comedy we usually parody something that's not a parody. Like how I parodied the science fiction fantasy *Star Wars* with *Spaceballs*. Or how *Scary Movie* by The Wayans parodied the horror film *Scream*. But what is this? What do we call a parody of a parody?

RICK MORANIS

We call it The Schmaltz.

MEL BROOKS

The Schmaltz?

RICK MORANIS

Yes, it's like how The Force in *Star Wars* became
The Schwartz in *Spaceballs,* you take it a little bit
further and you--

MEL BROOKS

You almost get too much.

RICK MORANIS

Exactly. Schmaltz is the extra fat or the drippings in
Yiddish. Which also means 'too much' in movies.

John Candy, the hefty hilarious comedian who
played Barf, who was a parody of Chewbaca, joins:

JOHN CANDY

Personally, I think Schmaltz gets a bad rap.
It's delicious. And can go on anything.
Have you had it on french fries?

Joan Rivers, the searing wit who played Dot Matrix,
who was a parody of C-3PO, joins.

JOAN RIVERS
It's also kind of like what I said about doing jokes about Anne Frank. When you do these jokes, it makes people remember. That process of bringing something back doesn't have to be a serious one. What we say is all nonsense, but it helps keep the memory alive. Of me I mean. Not Anne Frank. I'm dead now, too. And it's tragic so many of you don't remember me, I would've killed on TikTok!

MEL BROOKS
Are you sure we don't want to redraft this section like how I rewound and fast-forwarded the VHS tape in *Spaceballs*? Come up with a different bit?

RICK MORANIS
Well, if we wanna get real Sci-Fi, we can have an AI do a Four Questions parody of *Spaceballs* instead?

MEL BROOKS
Yes, let's try that. I'm curious.

You

Can you please do a funny parody of Mel Brook's movie Spaceballs as if the characters are doing the four questions for the Jewish holiday of Passover in a Haggadah?

ChatGPT

[Scene opens in the grandiose throne room of Planet Passover, where Dark Helmet, surrounded by his entourage of ludicrously dressed minions, sits atop his throne shaped like a giant matzo.]

Dark Helmet: (In a booming voice) Alright, everyone! It's time for the annual Passover celebration! Bring forth the Space Haggadah!

[Colonel Sandurz, nervously clutching a hefty tome, approaches Dark Helmet and hands him the Space Haggadah.]

Dark Helmet: (Clears throat dramatically) Let's see here... Ah, yes! The Four Questions! Gather around, my fellow space travelers, it's time to embark on a cosmic journey through the mysteries of Passover!

[The minions gather eagerly, their absurd costumes clashing with the solemnity of the occasion.]

Dark Helmet: (In a melodramatic tone) Question one! Why is this night different from all other nights?

[The minions murmur amongst themselves, some scratching their heads in confusion.]

Colonel Sandurz: Um, sir, I think I know the answer to that one! It's because on this night, we eat unleavened bread, right?

Dark Helmet: Correct, Colonel! On this night, we refrain from eating leavened bread, for it symbolizes the haste with which our ancestors fled Egypt!

[Dark Helmet nods approvingly as the minions nod along, some with comically exaggerated expressions of understanding.]

Dark Helmet: (Continues) Question two! Why do we dip our herbs twice?

[The minions exchange puzzled glances, a few attempting to discreetly sniff their herbs.]

Dark Helmet: Anyone?

[After an awkward pause, Snotty, the flamboyant sidekick, tentatively raises his hand.]

Snotty: Um, because it's twice as tasty that way?

[Dark Helmet gives Snotty an incredulous look before facepalming dramatically.]

Dark Helmet: No, you nitwit! We dip our herbs once for the bitterness of slavery and once for the sweetness of freedom!

[Snotty shrugs sheepishly as the other minions nod in understanding, albeit with varying degrees of comprehension.]

Dark Helmet: (With exaggerated patience) Question three! Why do we recline while eating tonight?

[The minions look genuinely perplexed, some attempting awkward half-slumps in their seats.]

Dark Helmet: Come on, people! Think about it! Why do we recline?

[After a moment of awkward silence, Pizza the Hutt, a giant pizza-like creature, pipes up from the back of the room.]

Pizza the Hutt: Because it's more comfortable than sitting up straight?

[Dark Helmet throws his hands up in exasperation as the minions chuckle nervously.]

Dark Helmet: No, you overgrown dough ball! We recline to symbolize our newfound freedom and luxury after escaping slavery!

[The minions nod in mock understanding, a few surreptitiously adjusting their postures to mimic reclining.]

Dark Helmet: (With exaggerated enthusiasm) And finally, question four! Why do we eat this strange mixture of matzo and bitter herbs?

[The minions exchange hesitant glances, their faces a mixture of confusion and amusement.]

Dark Helmet: (Rolls his eyes) Seriously, people? It's because the matzo represents the haste of our

ancestors' departure from Egypt, and the bitter
herbs remind us of the bitterness of slavery!

[The minions nod in faux comprehension, some
stifling giggles as they try to maintain the illusion of
solemnity.]

Dark Helmet: (Clapping his hands) Well done,
everyone! Another successful Passover celebration
in the books! Now, let's dig in before the food gets
cold!

[Amidst laughter and chatter, the minions eagerly
begin to partake in the Passover feast, their absurd
antics adding a touch of comedic flair to the ancient
traditions of the holiday.]

MEL BROOKS
Not bad!

RICK MORANIS
Yeah, I say we fire this Dave Cowen guy, and go
with ChatGPT the rest of the way?

THE FOUR CHILDREN (Young Frankenstein)

Gene Wilder, who played Dr. Frederick Frankenstein, a descendant of the original Dr. Frankenstein who reanimated the dead, but who starts the 1974 horror comedy parody, *Young Frankenstein*, as a scientific rationalist who doesn't believe in the occult, joins your table:

GENE WILDER
In *Young Frankenstein* my title character is so embarrassed about his family history that he changes the pronunciation of his name from the traditional Frankenstein. To something less recognizable: Franken steen.

Cloris Leachman, who played Frau Blucher, who was in love with Gene's forefather before he died and wants to reanimate his brain next, joins:

CLORIS LEACHMAN
He's not the first or the last to change the
pronunciation of their name seemingly to avoid
prejudice, is he?

GENE WILDER
Yes, I believe the author's family at some point
changed the pronunciation of their name to Cowen
as in Kau-uhn like Cow in. And not Cowen as in
Kow-uhn like Koh en.

CLORIS LEACHMAN
How's that going for you in 5784/2024?

DAVE COWEN
Um. Well. Some people who don't know me have
always called me Koh en instead of Cow in. But I
always hated being called Koh en. And also
sometimes my own Jewishness.

Gene Wilder & Cloris Leachman give each other a
Knew It look.

DAVE COWEN

But now. After October 7th. Most people when they
meet me. They call me Koh en. And if I try to
correct them to Cow in. They just continue to call
me Koh en. So I haven't been correcting them.
And I also identify with my Jewishness more.

GENE WILDER

It's almost like most Jews are like Dr. Frankenstein.
We can't escape our own history and lot either.

CLORIS LEACHMAN

It's your fate, Kohen! Your destiny! To not hide
behind a silly Irish or British sounding surname.

GENE WILDER

Say it. You are not Cowen.
You are Kohen.

DAVE COWEN

It's true.
I am a priest who has written 6 Haggadahs!

GENE WILDER
Pseudo-priest.

DAVE COWEN
Sorry. Right. A half comedy writer half priest.

CLORIS LEACHMAN
Half of a comedy writer too.

DAVE COWEN
Fine. I am a pseudo-priest / pseudo-comedy writer.
And I shall now forever be known again as. Dave-

GENE WILDER
David.

DAVID COWEN
David (Kohen)!

GENE WILDER
Great. You're still **The Wicked Child** for writing
this. So we'll blunt your teeth from speaking more
in this book. You know who is **The Good Child**?

CLORIS LEACHMAN
The reanimated creature in *Young Frankenstein*?!

Peter Boyle, who played the reanimated
creature/monster, and couldn't articulate a word
the audience could understand in the film, calls out!

PETER BOYLE
(mnuhanhhhh)

GENE WILDER
Him? No. See. I love him. Like a son. But he's
clearly **The Simple One**. Also honestly. **The One
Who Doesn't Know How To Ask A Question**.

MEL BROOKS
So who is **The Good Child**?

GENE WILDER
Me! For convincing you to direct this movie of my
idea! And to keep our legendary parody of Fred
Astaire's dance of "Puttin on the Ritz" in it!

65

MEL BROOKS

Do any of you children remember that?

The children at your table may or may not look dumbfounded, maybe even you, too.

In agony, Gene Wilder and Peter Boyle both let out the same unintelligible cry:

GENE WILDER   PETER BOYLE
(mnuhanhhhh)   (mnuhanhhhh)

MEL BROOKS

Well, let's at least make sure the kids continue to remember The Magid, the Exodus story, which is the real reason we get together for Passover, and is coming up next!

THE MAGID/EXODUS (History of the World: Part 1 and 2)

Mel, who played Moses in *History of the World: Part 1*, joins your table again.

MEL BROOKS

As you can tell, I was pretty obsessed with history. Not only did I do the longstanding sketch with Carl Reiner about the *2000 Year Old Man* but I also did a parody of history again in the movie *History of the World: Part 1*, with yes, some sketches about Moses. The most famous probably being when I brought out three stone tablets. And declared, "All you people, the Lord, the Lord Jehovah, has given unto you these 15--

One of the three tablets drops and breaks.

MEL BROOKS

Oy.

10 Commandments!

For all to obey.

Orson Welles, who played the narrator in *History of The World: Part 1*, joins your table.

ORSON WELLES

But that wasn't the only material on Moses you wrote and performed was it? You had The Magid/Exodus in there too right?

Mel looks at your table, sheepish.

MEL BROOKS

Well, sort of, there was a little gag we tacked on to the Roman section where Moses parted the sea for a standup philosopher Comicus and his friends.

The 2000 Year Old Man returns.

THE 2000 YEAR OLD MAN

Does that mean you're bringing me and this sketch from the beginning of the Haggadah back to fill in the gaps? Where did we leave off?

The 5784 Year Old Mother returns as well then.

THE 5784 YEAR OLD MOTHER
You weren't letting me tell you any of the details
about my relationship with Moses's brother, Aaron.

NICK KROLL
For good reason.

Nick Kroll, who helped carry the torch of *History of the World* into a *Part II* as a limited series for Hulu with David Stassen, Ike Barinholtz, Wanda Sykes, Mel Brooks, and many more, in 5783/2023, and played Judas as a parody of Larry David as well as Judas as a parody of The Beatles, and many more characters, joins your table.

THE 2000 YEAR OLD MAN
Now this is getting confusing. You're Nick Kroll who played Judas as a parody of Larry David and Judas as a parody of The Beatles in *History of the World: Part II*, and now you're in this parody written by someone else of the Magid as what now?

69

NICK KROLL
Still Judas.
Little known fact. Did you know The Last Supper
was a Passover Seder?
Even littler known fact. I wasn't The Wicked Child.
It was the other Judas. Judas Thaddeus.

MEL BROOKS
Huh. There was another Judas? Now that could be
a whole other mistaken identity sketch right there!

THE 2000 YEAR OLD MAN
I'm appalled. Judas jokes? At a Seder? In a
Passover Haggadah? Now *that* is a betrayal.

THE 5784 YEAR OLD MOTHER
What's next? Jesus here, too?

Moses joins the table.

MOSES
Nope, just me, Moses.

MEL BROOKS

The real Moses?

MOSES

I guess so.

Jesus appears too.

JESUS

Actually. Me, too.

Ike Barinholtz appears too.

IKE BARINHOLTZ

We're not supposed to say that these days!

Jesus, Jesus!

MEL BROOKS

Oy vey. Moses and Jesus at the same Seder.

In a parody Haggadah of me. That I didn't write.

This is bad enough.

What if that other guy shows up?

Pharoah appears too.

PHARAOH

Who me?

MEL BROOKS

No. Well. I meant the other other guy.

Who shares the same forefathers as us.

IKE BARINHOLTZ

The one we can't say's name, right?

Wanda Sykes appears too.

WANDA SYKES

Some of my people can say his name and be fine.

Kyrie. Kanye. Kareem.

Suddenly, Voldemort from *Harry Potter* appears.

VOLDEMORT

Who me?

NICK KROLL

No, not the villain in *Harry Potter* whose

characters refuse to say his name, we mean--

MEL BROOKS

No, no, Nick Kroll, let's go with this guy.

As a stand in. No need for extra trouble.

Mel holds his hands in prayer, looks to the sky.

MEL BROOKS

Humbly. We ask.

G-d, why have you brought us all here?

To tell a special version of the Magid?

In 5784/2024?

MOSES

Is it because our people have recently had a new

Mitzrayim, our people held hostage again? And

we asked those hostage-takers to let our people go,

let our people go, let our people go, we said, or else

modern plagues will befall them?

JESUS
Or is it because we have become a power structure
itself that oppresses and creates Mitzrayim or
suffering as well somewhat and sometimes? And we
need a revivication from within our people to open
our Pharoah-like hearts and stop us from hurting
another group we have dominion over?

VOLDEMORT
Or is it because both and many people have
forgotten the mystical elements of their religions,
that there is as much in common with Jewish
Kabbalah and Muslim Sufism and Christian
Contemplation, as there is with any form of magic,
which is just another name for you, dear G-d?

Suddenly, G-d appears.

G-D
You expect to find the answers here?
Written by this or any heretical humorist?

DAVID COWEN
Maybe not.

G-D
Good. Now then. Cut the jokes. And read the
plagues I gave to Pharaoh. And read them straight.
Or else I'll drop even worse plagues on you, you
un-G-d-fearing unfunny non-golden boy cow!

EVERYONE
The **Ten Plagues** were, are, will always be: **DAM**,
turning Egyptians water into blood;
TZFARDEAH, releasing frogs; **KINIM**, lice;
AROV, wild beasts; **DEVER**, diseasing livestock;
SH'HIN, boils; **BARAD**, hail; **ARBEH**, locusts;
HOSHEKH, darkness three days; and, **MAKAT
B'KHOROT**, the killing of firstborns.

Mel can't help himself, with a twist on "It's good to
be the King" from *History of the World*...

MEL BROOKS
It's good to be The Holy One, Blessed Be He!

THE IN EVERY GENERATION (Blazing Saddles)

Cleavon Little and Gene Wilder, who played Sheriff Bart and Jim The Waco Kid, respectively, in Mel's 1974 satire of Westerns, *Blazing Saddles*, join you.

CLEAVON LITTLE

I guess it's true what they say about In Every Generation?

GENE WILDER

What's that, Cleavon?

CLEAVON LITTLE

In Every Generation, there are Jewish comedy writers who rise up to satirize society as if they're the first one to do it and it might solve something.

GENE WILDER

You reckon they still think using the most racist words in the language like we did is still funny?

CLEAVON LITTLE

Let's find out? But instead of the word that starts with a N for my black people, let's try...

EVERYONE:

Not only one enemy has risen against us, but **In Every Generation** there are those who will rise against the *Kikes*. G-d promised and promises to deliver us *Kikes* from those who seek *Kike* harm with a mighty hand and an outstretched arm, miraculous signs and wonders. At the very least G-d gives us *Kikes* an iron dome, one of the best militaries in the world, and hopefully not too much *Kike* power to accidentally cause us to be our own worst enemy and undoing, or something like that, wow, saying *Kike* this much, really puts things in perspective, maybe it isn't such a good idea to use insulting words, even ironically, or combine humor with politics, and think you can be right, not self-righteous, when it's so complex, sorry to anyone offended, maybe the next generation will finally do things better, yet still be funny, good luck!

THE MIRIAM CUP/THE SECOND CUP OF WINE (To Be Or Not To Be)

Mel Brooks and Anne Bancroft, who were happily married for many years, co-starred in one Brooksfilm production in 1983 as husband and wife, a remake of the 1942 original war comedy by German-Jewish-American immigrant director, Ernst Lubitsch, *To Be Or Not To Be,* in which a Polish troop of play actors is put in a position to use their acting abilities to fool the invading Nazis.

MEL BROOKS
Who else to do The Miriam Cup, which is a special extra glass of wine dedicated to Moses's sister and women everywhere, but my talented, smart, lovely, beautiful wife, Anne Bancroft, who--

ANNE BANCROFT
Is Italian, not even Jewish, and way better looking than you...but loved you very much.

MEL BROOKS

And didn't have affairs like your character, Anna
Bronski, did in *To Be Or Not To Be*, on her poor
husband, me, Frederick Bronski, with younger,
handsomer, more "Alpha," admirers?

ANNE BANCROFT

Art could never imitate our life, Mel.

MEL BROOKS

So that's a no, right? That's a no on the affair.

Anne raises a glass, paraphrases a line from the film

ANNE BANCROFT

To life. We give our greatest performances. And
almost nobody sees it. Except G-d. L'Chayim!

MEL BROOKS

You still...You still haven't fully answered no about
the affairs.

Anne kisses Mel, then feeds him his glass of wine.

ANNE BANCROFT
Just say the prayer, silly.

EVERYONE:

בָּרוּךְ אַתָּה יְיָ אֱלוֹהֵינוּ מֶלֶךְ הָעוֹלָם,
בּוֹרֵא פְּרִי הַגָּפֶן.

Baruch atah Ad-nai, Eloheinu Melech ha'olam,
bo're p'ri hagafen.

Praised are You, our G-d, who blesses us and
creates the fruit of the vine.

DAYEINU (High Anxiety)

Mel is back, this time as Dr. Richard Harpo
Thorndyke from his 1977 parody of Alfred
Hitchcock movies and psychotherapy *High Anxiety*.

MEL BROOKS
In my Hitchcock parody, *High Anxiety,* I play a
psychiatrist trying to uncover malfeasance and
malpractice at a mental hospital I've taken over as
the head of, but ironically I suffer from my own
neurosis, most specifically, a fear of heights.

Madeline Kahn who played Victoria Brisbane joins.

MADELINE KAHN
I play the beautiful daughter of an inmate who
teams up with you. And. Falls in love with you.

Cloris Leachman and Harvey Korman, who played
Charlotte Diesel and Dr. Charles Montague, the two
villains, respectively, join your table as well.

CLORIS LEACHMAN

And we played mental hospital administrators and
secret lovers and S&M fetishists.

HARVEY KORMAN

Who were also just plain sadists in the traditional
sense of the word in their jobs, terrorizing patients.

MEL BROOKS

Sometimes I think about what it must have been
like to be Pharaoh. Finally, you let Moses and the
Jewish people leave. Your institution of slavery. But
then no. You masochistically chase after them. To
the Red Sea. Even though Moses tells you what will
happen if you follow, you masochistically continue
after. Then the sea parts to let the Jews cross. But
you and your Egyptian army are wiped out of
existence by it. Why would someone let their
masochism devolve into their utter destruction?

HARVEY KORMAN

While we have never studied psychology.

CLORIS LEACHMAN

Or been to therapy.

HARVEY KORMAN

We have been actors in a parody of a Sub and
Master relationship. We theorize that...

CLORIS LEACHMAN

Pharaoh didn't know G-d's safe word.

MADELINE KAHN

Wow. Huh. And, what was that word?

MEL BROOKS

Of course. **Dayeinu**! Enough. Never said enough!

HARVEY KORMAN

It's just a theory.

CLORIS LEACHMAN

But it's enough for a PhD. And for us to make a new
mental hospital. Or at least a sequel.

83

THE RAHTZAH and MOTZI-MATZAH-MAROR-KORECH (Other Brookses)

MEL BROOKS
OK, who is hungry? Are we ready to wash our hands of this Haggadah? Should we **Ratzah** it? Which is the second washing of the hands with a prayer this time?

EVERYONE:

בָּרוּךְ אַתָּה ה', אֱ-לֹהֵינוּ מֶלֶךְ הָעוֹלָם, אֲשֶׁר קִדְּשָׁנוּ בְּמִצְוֹתָיו, וְצִוָּנוּ עַל נְטִילַת יָדָיִם.

Baruch atah Ad-nai, Eloheinu Melech ha`olam, asher kid'shanu b'mitzvotav v'tzivanu `al netilat yadayim.

Praised are You, our G-d, who blesses us and instructs us to wash our hands.

MEL BROOKS

Sometimes at the end of my stuff, I did bits about what's next, like coming attractions, without those things ever coming, I might have been the one to start that? Who knows? What are some other things you could have had Mel Brooksian parodies about?

DAVE COWEN

I had this idea, kind of similar to how The **Motzi** is the first blessing over the Matzo and then it's followed by **Matzah**, which is the second blessing over the Matzo.

MEL BROOKS

Hold on a moment.

Everyone say those prayers!

85

EVERYONE:

בָּרוּךְ אַתָּה ה', אֱ-לֹהֵינוּ מֶלֶךְ
הָעוֹלָם, הַמּוֹצִיא לֶחֶם מִן
הָאָרֶץ.

Baruch atah Ad-nai, Eloheinu Melech ha'olam,
hamotzi lechem min ha'aretz.

Praised are You, our G-d, who blesses us and
brings forth bread from the land.

EVERYONE:

בָּרוּךְ אַתָּה יְיָ, אֱלֹהֵינוּ מֶלֶךְ הָעוֹלָם,
אֲשֶׁר קִדְּשָׁנוּ בְּמִצְוֹתָיו וְצִוָּנוּ עַל
אֲכִילַת מַצָּה

Baruch atah Ad-nai, Eloheinu Melech ha'olam,
asher kid-shanu b'mitzvotav v'tzivanu al achilat
matzah.

Praised are You, our G-d, who blesses us and
instructs us to eat matzo.

MEL BROOKS

OK, what were you saying? I was riveted.

DAVE COWEN

That we should double down on the end like those
double prayers and do Mel Brooksian parodies
about other Hollywood Brookses?

MEL BROOKS

Who? My son, Max? The writer of *World War Z*?

DAVE COWEN

I was thinking Albert and James L. Brooks. Your
films are pretty much all broad comedies. While
theirs, like Albert's *Lost in America*, *Modern
Romance*, or *Defending Your Life*, or James L.'s *As
Good As It Gets*, *Terms of Endearment*, and
Broadcast News, are kind of a beautiful mixture of
funny and serious. Like the **Korech** sandwich.
Which combines **Maror**, the bitter herb, with the
Charoset, the sweet mixture, into a bittersweet
sandwich to eat, the last ritual before the meal,
signifying the bittersweetness of life.

Mel considers this, as he passes the Korech
sandwiches out to your table, the last ritual before
you can eat your meal, but then says:

MEL BROOKS
Didn't James L. Brooks make *The Simpsons?*

DAVE COWEN
He didn't create it. But he did executive produce--

MEL BROOKS
Now *The Simpsons*. That'd be a good Haggadah.
Has anyone done that yet? Hurry up, let these poor
people say their prayer and eat their Korech, and be
done with this one, so they finally eat their meal.

THE 5784 YEAR OLD MOTHER
I was talking to your mother the other day, David.
She said, Stop bothering people with these books.

DAVID COWEN
Oy vey.

EVERYONE:

בָּרוּךְ אַתָּה יי אֱלֹהֵינוּ מֶלֶךְ הָעוֹלָם,
אֲשֶׁר קִדְּשָׁנוּ בְּמִצְוֹתָיו וְצִוָּנוּ עַל
אֲכִילַת מָרוֹר

*Baruch atah Ad-nai, Eloheinu Melech ha'olam,
asher kid'shanu b'mitzvotav v'tzivanu al achilat
maror.*

*Praised are You, our G-d, who blesses us and
instructs us to eat maror.*

Everyone eats their Korech sandwich.

SHULCHAN OREICH (Brooklyn)

MEL BROOKS

It's time for the meal. Don't forget to thank your hosts! I grew up in Brooklyn, New York, around the time of The Great Depression, and mostly without a father, who died when we were young.

We sometimes could barely afford anything. Including tickets to High Holidays. Which wasn't so bad I thought back then. But as you get older, you realize these gatherings don't always happen.

So don't take them or anyone in your life for granted. Practice the joy of gratitude. As you Shulchan Oreich. And ENJOY YOUR MEAL!!!

THE NIRZAH (World Wars)

DAVE COWEN
Well, that's it. A 6th Haggadah in the books.

MEL BROOKS
This is the time where we say Next Time In
Jerusalem, right?

DAVE COWEN
Yeah.

MEL BROOKS
Have you ever been to Jerusalem? To Israel?

DAVE COWEN
I haven't. But. I did go to Berlin. To Germany.
For the first time ever in December 5783/2023.

MEL BROOKS
You went to Berlin before Jerusalem? What kind of
Jewish-American putz--

DAVE COWEN

I know. I know. But. I've got to say. It was after
October 7th. And I had never been there before.
But I felt a major vibe shift.

MEL BROOKS

A major what? What do you mean?

DAVE COWEN

My name, at hotels, or museums. David Cowen.
Everyone knew I was Jewish.

MEL BROOKS

So what? Did you fear for your life or something?

DAVE COWEN

Yes. Sometimes. I can get very anxious.
There was Palestine and Gaza graffiti everywhere.
The point is: I got this sense that they were looking
at me. At us. Jews. Like.
You're not so special? You can be oppressors too?
You know?

MEL BROOKS

Hm.

I don't know either.

First of all, I was a US soldier in World War 2.

Not a Holocaust survivor.

Second of all, I am you writing as me.

But I think a genocide is when a people isn't

fighting back at all.

There were no Jewish militants, attacking

Germans.

But there were and are Hamas militants, attacking

Jews.

DAVE COWEN

I guess that makes me feel better.

But.

Their faces. The Germans. I can see them now.

It was almost like. They were also saying.

Don't become us?

The oppressor goes through as much pain, in the

end, as the oppressed?

93

MEL BROOKS
I wish I could say I knew the answer, Mr. Cowen.

But.

The only answer I have is.

Keep asking questions.

DAVE COWEN
And keep writing Haggadahs?

MEL BROOKS
I don't know about that either, son.

Mel winks, his eyes twinkling, with that
quintessential yet archetypal impish grin of his.

MEL BROOKS
Chag Sameach!

THE SPOOF SEDER HAGGADAH: A Passover Parody of Mel Brooks Parodies!

Is written as a parody of the work of Mel Brooks and as a teaching tool for Judaism.

It is not authorized or endorsed by him or any of the other writers, producers, actors, or any of the companies or corporations involved in its production and distribution.

Hebrew as well as English transliteration open-sourced from various online sources.

It also references Mel's autobiography *All About Me!*

A portion of the profits will go to the State of Israel as well as a Jewish organization that wants a peaceful end to the current conflict in 2024.

Thank you in eternal gratitude to G-d, my family, friends, and you the people who enjoy these books.

Made in the USA
Monee, IL
27 June 2024